THE
REAL
MAN

A Study Guide

Kristen D. Hall

WESTBOW
PRESS°
A DIVISION OF THOMAS NELSON
& ZONDERVAN

WestBow Press books may be ordered through
booksellers or by contacting:

WestBow Press
A Division of Thomas Nelson & Zondervan
1663 Liberty Drive
Bloomington, IN 47403
www.westbowpress.com
1 (866) 928-1240

Because of the dynamic nature of the Internet, any web addresses or
links contained in this book may have changed since publication and
may no longer be valid. The views expressed in this work are solely those
of the author and do not necessarily reflect the views of the publisher,
and the publisher hereby disclaims any responsibility for them.

Any people depicted in stock imagery provided by Thinkstock are models,
and such images are being used for illustrative purposes only.
Certain stock imagery © Thinkstock.

ISBN: 978-1-4908-9421-8 (sc)
ISBN: 978-1-4908-9422-5 (e)

Print information available on the last page.

WestBow Press rev. date: 08/24/2015

TABLE OF CONTENTS

CHAPTER 1

GOD IS A triune being God is a spirit. John 4:24. God has a soul or heart. Behold my servant, whom I have chosen; my beloved, in whom my soul is well pleased: I will put my spirit upon him, and he shall shew judgment to the Gentiles. Matt. 12:18. The Lord hath sought him a man after his own heart. 1 Sam. 13:14. I have found David the son of Jesse, a man after my own heart. Acts 13:22. God has a body. His body is the Lord Jesus Christ. And the word was made flesh and dwelt among us (and we beheld his glory the glory of the only begotten of the Father) full of grace and truth. John 1:14.

Man is a triune being. And God said, let us make man in our image after our likeness. Gen. 1:26. And the Lord formed man of the dust of the ground and breathed into his nostrils the breath of life: and man became a living soul (heart). Gen 2:17. Breath in Hebrew out of Strong's Concordance is mes-aw-mah (5397) which means spirit or inspiration. Soul or heart in Hebrew out of Strong's Concordance is neh-fesh (5315) which means breathing creature, i.e. animal or vitality. It also means any appetite, desire, person, pleasure, mind, heart and will. And man was formed of the dust of the ground which means man has a body. Man is a soul (heart), spirit and body just like God.

God fashioned woman from man. And the Lord said, It is not good that man should be alone; I will make him an help meet for him. Gen. 2:18. And the Lord caused a deep sleep to fall upon Adam, and he slept. And he took one of his ribs and closed up the flesh instead thereof; and the rib, which the Lord God had taken from man, made he a woman, and he brought her unto the man. And Adam said, This is now bone of my bones, and flesh of my ;flesh: she was called woman. Gen. 2:21-23. In Hebrew bone is eh-teem (6106) which means body, substance or selfsame. According to Funk and Wagnell's Standard Desk Dictionary selfsame means exactly the same; identical. Woman was made identical to man meaning she was a triune being. She was made with refinement as she wasn't formed out of dust.

Let's examine the soul. The soul is found in the blood. For the life of the flesh is in the blood: and I have given it to you upon the altar to make atonement for your souls: for it is the blood that maketh an atonement for the soul. Lev. 17:11. And whatsoever man there be of the children of Israel, or of the strangers that sojourn among you, which hunteth and catcheth any beast or fowl that may be eaten; he shall pour out the blood thereof, and cover it with dust. For it is for the life thereof; therefore I said unto the children of Israel, ye shall eat the blood of no manner of flesh: for the life of all flesh is in the blood thereof. Gen. 9:4. Only be sure that thou eat not the blood; for the blood; for the blood is the life; and thou mayest not eat the life of the flesh. Deut. 12:23. The word life in Hebrew from Strong's Concordance is neh-fesh

(5315) which also means soul 5315. The soul and life are defined as a breathing creature, animal, life or vitality. It also means any appetite, desire, person, heart, will and mind. It is the soul that is the life of the flesh and it is found in the blood. Here is a list of scriptures from the Old Testament where 5315 proves life and soul are the same thing.

Life	5315.	2 Sam.	1:9
Ge.	9: 4, 5		4:8
	19:17, 19		14:7
	32:30		16:11
	44:30		18:13
	45:5		19:5
Ex.	4:19	1 Ki.	1:12, 12
	21:23, 30		2:23
Le.	17:11, 14, 14, 14		3:11
De.	12:23, 23		19:2, 3, 4, 10, 14
	19:21		20:31, 39, 42
	20:19	2 Ki.	1:13, 14
	24:6		7:7
Jos.	2:14		10:24
J'g.	12:2	2 Ch.	1:11
	18:25	Es.	7:3, 7
Ru.	4:15		8:11
1 Sam.	19:5	Job	2:4, 6
	20:1		6:11
	22:23		13:14
	23:15	Ps.	31:13
	26:24, 24		38:12
	28:9, 21	Pr.	1:19

	6:26		30:12
	12:10	**Le.**	4:2
	13:3, 8		5:1, 2, 4, 15,17
Isa.	15:4		6:2
	43:4		7:18, 20,20, 21, 21,
Jer.	4:30		25, 27, 27
	11:21		17:10, 11, 12, 15
	21:7, 9		19:8
	22:25		20:6, 6
	34:20, 21		22:3, 6, 11
	38:2, 16		23:29, 30,30
	39:18		26:11, 15, 30, 43
	44:30, 30	**Nu.**	9:13
	45:5		11:6
	49:37		15:27, 28, 30, 30,
La.	2:19		31
Eze.	32:10		19:13, 20, 22
Jo.	1:14		21:4, 5
	4:3		30:2, 4, 4, 5, 6, 7,
			8, 10, 11, 12, 13
Soul	**5315.**		31:28
Ge.	2:7	**De.**	4:9, 29
	12:13		6:5
	17:14		10:12
	19:20		11:13, 18
	27:4, 19,25, 31		12:15, 20,20
	34:3, 8		14:26, 26
	38:18		26:16
	42:21		30:2, 6, 10
	49:6	**Jos.**	4:9, 29
Ex.	13:15, 19	**J'g.**	5:21

Ec.	2:24		6:8
	4:8		9:9
	6:2, 3		12:7
	7:28		13:17
SofS.	1:7		14:19
	3:1, 2, 3, 4		18:20
	5:6		20:13
	6:12		31:12, 14, 25, 25
Isa.	1:14		32:41
	3:9		38:16, 17, 20
	10:18		50:19
	26:8,, 9	La.	1:11, 16
	29:8, 8		2:12
	32:15, 17		3:17, 20, 24, 25, 58
	38:15, 17	Eze.	3:19,21
	42:1		11:14
	44:20		18:4, 4, 4, 20, 27
	51:23		24:21
	53:10, 11, 12		33:5, 9
	55:2, 3	Ho.	9:4
	58:3, 5, 10, 10, 11	Jo.	2:5, 7
	61:10	Mic.	6:7
	66:3		7:1
Jer.	4:10, 19, 31	Hab.	2:4, 10
	5:9	Zec.	11:8, 8

The New Testament supports the conclusion that the soul means life. In the Greek from Strong's Concordance life and soul is psoo-khay (5590) which means spirit, the rational and immortal soul, life, vitality, mind, heart, us, you. Funk and Wagnell's Standard Desk Dictionary give the definition of life as a living being; person. The soul is the life of the flesh. The following scriptures proves the life to be the soul.

Life	5590	Soul	5590
M't.	2:20	M't.	10:28
	6:25, 25		16:28, 28
	10:39, 39		223:37
	16:25, 25	M'r.	12:30, 33
	20:28	Lu.	1:46
M'r.	3:4		2:35
	8;35, 35		10:37
	10:45	Ac.	2:43
Lu.	6:9		3:23
	9:24. 24		4:22
	12:22, 23	Ro.	2:9
	14:26		13:1
	17:33, 33	2 Cor.	1:23
Jo.	10:11, 15	1 Th.	5:23
	12:25, 25	Heb.	4:12
	15:13		6:19
Ac.	27:22		10:38
Ro	1:3	3 Jo.	2
	16:4	Rev.	16:3
Ph'p.	2:30		18:4
1 Jo.	3:16		
Rev.	8:9		

CHAPTER 2

ANOTHER TRAIT OF the soul is the will. It has been taught that the will resides in the brain. According to the Bible the will is part of the soul. In the Hebrew will is neh-fesh (5315) in Strong's Concordance. It is defined to be a breathing creature, i.e. animal or vitality. It also means any appetite, desire, person, will and mind. Soul 5315 means the same thing. Funk and Wagnell's Standard Desk Dictionary defines will as that which has been resolved or determined upon; a purpose. The following is a list of scriptures which relates soul to the will.

Will	5315		
De.	21:14, 18, 18, 20		32:5, 8, 8
	23:21		34:1, 11
Ps.	27:12		35:18, 18
	28:1, 7		37:33
	29:11, 11		38:18, 18
	30:1, 12		39:1, 1
	31:7		41:2, 2
			42:6, 8, 9

116:2, 9, 13, 14,
    17, 17, 18
118:6, 10, 11, 19,
    21, 24, 28, 28
119:7, 8, 15, 16,
    32, 45, 46, 46,
    47, 48, 48, 62,
    69,
74, 78, 93, 95, 106,
    106, 115, 117,
    134, 145
121:1, 3, 3
122:8, 9
132:3, 4, 7, 7, 11,
    11, 12, 14, 15,
    15, 16, 17, 18
135:14, 14
138:1, 1, 2, 8
139:14
140:12
143:10

Pr.   10:8
12:2
14:5, 5
15:12, 25
16:14
18:14
19:6, 17, 24, 25
20:3, 4, 5, 6, 22

Soul 5315 has already been listed on pages 5-12.

CHAPTER 3

THE SOUL HAS another component called the heart. In Hebrew from Strong's Concordance heart is nehfesh (5315). The heart is full of blood (containing the soul) therefore it is part of the soul. The heart 5315 means breathing creature, animal or vitality. Heart is used widely in a lit. accommodated or fig. (bodily or mentally)-any appetite, desire, person, pleasure, mind, heart, will. The following is a list of scriptures that prove that the heart is a major component of the soul.

Heart	5315	Ho.	25:6
Ex.	23:9		
	24:15	Soul	5315.
1 Sam.	2:33		Ge. 2:7
2 Sam.	3:21		12:13
Pr.	23:17		17:14
	28:25		27:4, 19, 25, 31
La.	3:51		34:3, 8
Eze.	25:6		35:18

The soul and heart (5315) have many aspects and their definition is expansive. In Hebrew from Strong's Concordance the mind is neh-fesh (5315). The soul, heart and mind are defined to be a breathing creature, i.e. animal or vitality. They also means any appetite, desire, person, heart, will, and mind. Therefore it can be concluded that the mind is another interpretation of the soul and heart. The mind is part of the soul and heart. The following is a list of scriptures that prove the mind to be a part of the soul and heart.

Mind 5315
Gen.   23:8
De.   18:6
           28:65
1 Sam. 2:35
1 Ch. 28:9
Eze.   22:17, 18, 18, 22, 28

Soul 5315 has already been
listed on pages 5-12.

Heart 5315 has already been |
listed on page 18.

———————————————————————

Upon investigation of the New Testament the same truth is found. In the Greek the mind is psoo-khay (5590) which means spirit, the rational and immortal soul, vitality, life, mind, heart, us, you. The mind is part of the soul and heart.

———————————————————————

Mind 5590
Ph'p 1:27

Soul 5590 has already been
listed on pages 13-14.

Heart 5590
Eph.   6:6

CHAPTER 4

L ET'S VIEW SOME other aspects of the heart. In Hebrew from Strong's Concordance heart is labe (3820) which means feeling, the will, even intellect, mind and understanding. According to Funk and Wagnell's Standard Desk Dictionary feeling means emotion, a sensation of awareness of something. The will is that which has been resolved or determined upon; a purpose. It was found to be in the soul. Here we find it to be seated in the heart and is a part of the soul as well. The heart and soul are one as we have already been studied. The intellect, mind and understanding are the heart's ability too perceive and grasp ideas and concepts. The heart and mind are also found to mean the same thing. In the Hebrew from Strong's Concordance mind and heart are labe (3820) which has just been discussed. The following is a list of scriptures that connect the mind with the heart (3820).

Mind	**3820**	**Ru.**	3:7
Nu	16:28	**1 Sam.**	1:13
	24:13		2:1
1 Sam.	9:20		4:13
Ne.	4:6		17:52
Job	23:13		24:5
Pr.	21:27		25:31, 37
Isa.	46:8	**2 Sam.**	6:16
	65:17		7:27
Jer.	3:16		13:28, 33
	19:5		14:1
	32:35		17:10
	44:21		24:10
La.	3:21	**1 Ki.**	3:6, 9, 12
			4:29
Heart	**3820**		8:23, 66
Gen.	6:5, 6		9:3
	8:21, 21		10:24
Ex.	4:14		12:26, 27, 33
	25:2		18:37
	28:29		21:7
	35:5, 29, 35	**2 Ki.**	5:26
	36:2		6:11
Nu.	32:7		12:4
De.	28:65		23:3
	29:4, 19	**1 Ch.**	12:17, 33,38
Jos.	5:8		15:29
J'g.	5:15, 16		16:10
	16:6		28:9
	18:20	**2 Ch.**	6:38
	19:5, 6		7:10

	9:23		49:3
	12:14		51:17
	25:2, 19		57:7
	26:16		58:2
	29:34		61:2
	32:25, 26		66:18
Ne.	2:2		78:18
Es.	5:9		84:2
	6:6		101:5
	7:5		107:12
Job	17:11, 17		109:22
	29:13		111:1
	31:7, 9, 27		112:8
	33:3		119:32, 34, 36, 80,
	36:15		112, 145, 161
Ps.	10:11		131:1
	12:2		140:2
	13:5		143:4
	15:2	Pr.	3:1, 3, 5
	19:14		4:4
	22:14		6:18, 21, 25
	24:4		7:10, 25
	26:2		12:8, 23, 25
	27:3, 14		13:12
	28:7		14:13, 14, 30
	34:18		15:28
	37:31		16:1
	38:8, 10		18:2, 15
	41:6		19:3, 21
	44:21		20:5
	45:1		22:15, 17

	23:17, 19, 33		11:8, 18
	26:25		13:10
Ec.	2:10, 20, 22, 23		16:2
	5:2		17:5, 10
	7:2, 3, 4, 7, 26		18:12
	8:5, 9		23:16, 17, 20, 26
	9:1, 2, 2		30:24
	11:9, 9		48:31, 36
Isa.	33:10	**La.**	2:19
	35:4		11:19
	38:18		14:3
	44:19		18:31
	57:11		33:31
	59:13		36:26
	63:4	**Da.**	1:8
Jer.	3:15		2:30
	4:18, 19	**Ho.**	7:6
	5:23		10:2
	7:24		13:6, 8
	9:28		

The heart is further described in Hebrew from Strong's Concordance is lay-bawb (3824) which means the most interior, the heart, breast, mind and understanding. The heart and soul share the same meaning as it has been discovered with 5315 which means heart and soul. The heart is the most interior part of the soul. The dictionary defines interior as that which is situated on the inside; inner. The dictionary meaning of heart is the seat of emotion. The breast is defined as the seat of emotions. The heart is where understanding originates. Understanding is perception, the ability to lay hold of or grasp mentally. This is a function of the mind.

Upon studying Strong's Concordance from the Hebrew lay-bawb (3824) means heart and mind. The heart is the seat of the mind but the mind is also part of the soul. The mind is where thoughts, imaginations, feelings, memory, and desires take place. The following is a list of scriptures that relate the mind to the heart (3824).

Mind	**3824**		19:6
De.	30:1		28:28, 47, 67
1Ch.	22:7		29:18
Jer.	51:50		30:6, 17
Eze.	38:10	**Jos.**	5:1
Da.	2:29		22:5
			24:23
Heart	**3824**	**J'g.**	19:8, 9
Gen.	20:5, 6	**1 Sam.**	1:8
Le.	19:17		9:19
Nu.	15:39		12:20, 24
De.	1:28		13:14
	2:30		14:17
	4:9, 29		17:28
	6:5, 6		21:12
	8:2, 5	**2 Sam.**	7:3
	9:4, 5	**1 Ki.**	2:4, 44
	10:16		8:38, 39, 48, 61
	11:13, 16, 16		11:2, 9
	13:3		14:8
	15:7, 9, 10	**2 Ki.**	10:15

	14:10		27:6
	20:3	**Ps.**	4:4
	22:19		13:2
1 Ch.	12:38		22:26
	17:2, 24, 25		25:17
	22:19		73:1
	29:9, 17, 18, 19		95:10
2 Ch.	15:12, 15, 17		102:4
	16:9	**Pr.**	6:25
	19:3, 9	**Ec.**	
	22:9	**Isa.**	7:2
	29:31		9:9
	30:19		10:7, 12
	31:21		13:7
	32:31		21:4
	34:27	**Jer.**	4:4
Ne.	9:8	**La.**	5:17
Job	9:4	**Joel**	2:13
	10:13		

The heart has other descriptions found in Strong's Concordance. In the Hebrew heart is bawl (1079) which means the heart (as it's seat). Another definition in the Hebrew is leb-ab (3825) which means heart. According to Funk and Wagnell's Standard Desk Dictionary heart means the seat of emotion. It is the central or inner part of anything. Heart in Hebrew is law-bab (3823) which means to be enclosed, to unheart. Another Hebrew word for heart is lib-baw (3826) which means the heart. Heart is further described in Hebrew as sek-vee (7907) which means observant, the mind, heart. Finally the heart in Hebrew is keh-reb (7130) which means nearest part, i.e. centre, heart, within self. The heart is the center of the soul. It is the seat of the mind, will and emotions.

The heart has desires and is the seat of the mind, will and emotions. Many things take place in the heart. The following is a list of scriptures that describes the many attributes of the heart 1079, 5315, 3820, 3823, 3824, 3825, 3826, 7130 and 7907. Included are the reference numbers that coincide with Strong's Concordance.

Heart

Gen   6:5 thoughts of the heart (3820).

        6 grieved him at his heart (3820).

        8:21 Lord said in His heart (3820).

        21 imagination of man's heart is evil (3820).

        20:5 integrity of thy heart (3824).

        5 integrity of thy heart (3824).

Ex.   4:14 gladness (3820).

        25:2 willingly (3820).

        28:29 judgment (3820).

        35:5 willingly (3820).

        29 willingly (3820).

        30:2 wisdom of the heart (3820).

        36:2 wisdom (3820).

Le.   19:17 hate (3824).

        26:16 sorrow (5315).

Nu.   15:39 seek (3824).

        32:7 discourage (3820).

        9 discourage (3820).

De. 1:28 discourage (3824).

2:30 obstinate (3824).

4:9 seek (3824).

29 consider (3824).

6:5 love (3824).

6 words (3824).

5 consider (3824).

9:4 speak (3824).

5 uprightness (3824).

10:16 foreskin (3824).

11:13 serve (3824).

16 deception (3824).

16 words (3824).

13:3 love (3824).

15:7 harden (3824).

9 thought (3824).

10 grief (3824).

19:6 hot (3824).

28:28 blindness and astonishment (3824).

47 joyfulness and gladness (3824).

65 trembling (3820).

67 fear (3824).

29:4 perceive (3820).

19 imagination (3820).

30:6 circumcise (3824).

17 turn away (3824).

Jos. 5:1 melted (3824).

8 melt (3824).

22:5 serve (3824).

24:23 incline (3824).

J'g. 5:1 thoughts (3820).

16 searching (3820).

16:6 told (3820).

18:20 glad (3820).

19:5 comfort (3824).

6 merry (3820).

8 comfort (3824).

9 merry (3820).

Ru. 3:7 merry (3920).

1 Sam. 1:8 grieved (3824).

13 spake (3820).

2:1 rejoiced (3820).

33 grieved (5315).

4:13 trembled (3820).

9:19 tell (3824).

12:20 serve (3824).

24 serve (3824).

13:14 sought (3824).

17:28 naughtiness (3824).

52 fail (3820).

21:12 words (3824).

24:5 smote (3820).

25:31 offense (3820).

37 merry (3820).

28:5 trembled (3820).

2 Sam. 3:21 desireth (5315).

6:16 despised (3820).

7:3 do (3824).

27 found to pray (3820).

13:28 merry (3820).

33 take (3820).

14:1 toward (3820).

24:10 smote (3820).

1 Ki. 2:44 wickedness (3824).

3:6 uprightness (3820).

9 understanding (3820).

12 wise and understanding (3829).

5:29 largeness (3820).

8:23 walk (3820).

38 plague (3824).

39 knowest (3824).

48 return (3824).

61 perfection (3824).

66 glad (3820).

9:3 eyes of mine heart (3820).

4 integrity (3824).

10:24 wisdom (3820).

11:2 turn away (3824).

9 turned (3824).

12:26 said (3820).

27 turn (3824).

33 devised (3820).

14:8 followed (3824).

18:37 turned (3820).

2 Ki. 6:11 sore (3820).

10:15 right (3824).

12:4 cometh (3824).

14:10 lifted thee up (3824).

20:3 perfect (3824).

22:19 tender (3824).

1 Ch. 12:17 knit (3820).

33 double (3820).

38 perfect (3824).

38 one (3820).

15:29 despised (3820).

16:10 rejoice (3820).

17:2 do (3824).

24 found to pray (3824).

25 found to pray (3824).

17 uprightness (3824).

18 thoughts (3824).

19 perfect (3824).

2 Ch. 6:38 return (3820).

7:10 merry (3820).

9:23 wisdom (3820).

12:14 seek (3820).

15 sworn (3824).

17 perfect (3824).

16:9 perfect (3824).

19:3 seek (3824).

9 perfect (3824).

22:9 sought (3824).

25:2 perfect (3820).

19 lifts up (3820).

26:16 lifts up (3820).

29:31 free (3824).

34 upright (3820).

30:19 seek (3824).

31:21 prospered (3824).

32:25 lifted up (3820).

26 pride (3820).

31 know (3824).

34:27 tender (3824).

Ne.   2:2 sorrow (3820).

9:8 faithful (3824).

Es.   5:9 joyful and glad (3820).

6:6 thought (3820).

7:5 presume (3820).

Job   9:4 wise (3824).

10:13 hid (3824).

17:4 understanding (3820).

11 thoughts (3820).

27:6 reproach (3824).

29:13 sing (3820).

9 deceived (3820).

27 enticed (3820).

33:3 uprightness (3820).

36:15 heap up wrath (3820).

Ps.   4:4 commune (3824).

10:11 forgotten (3820).

12:2 double (3820).

13:2 soul having sorrow in my heart (3824).

5 rejoice (3820).

15:2 speaketh (3820).

19:14 meditation of my heart (3820).

22:14 like wax it is melted (3820).

26 live forever (3824).

24:4 pure (3820).

25:17 troubles (3824).

26:2 reins (3820).

27:3 fear (3820).

14 strengthen (3820).

28:7 trusted (3820).

34:18 broken (3820).

37:31 law of God (3820).

38:8 disquietness (3820).

10 panteth (3820).

41:6 gathereth iniquity (3820).

44:21 knoweth secrets (3820).

45:1 inditing (3820).

49:3 meditation (3820).

51:17 broken and contrite (3820).

57:7 fixed (3820).

58:2 work wickedness (3820).

61:2 overwhelmed (3820).

66:18 regard iniquity (3820).

73:1 clean (3824).

78:18 tempted God (3820).

84:2 crieth out (3820).

95:10 do err in heart (3824).

101:4 froward (3824).

5 proud (3820).

102:4 smitten (3824).

107:12 brought down (3820).

109:22 wounded (3820).

111:1 whole heart (3820).

112:8 established (3820).

119:32 enlarge (3820).

34 observe (3820).

36 incline (3820).

80 be sound (3820).

112 inclined to perform (3820).

145 cried (3820).

161 standeth in awe (3820).

131:1 haughty (3820).

140:2 imagine mischiefs (3820).

143:4 desolate (3820).

Pr. 3:1 keep my commandments (3820).

5 trust (3820).

4:4 retain (3820).

6:18 deviseth wicked (3820).

21 bind (3820).

25 beauty (3824).

7:10 subtle (3820).

25 decline (3820).

12:8 perverse (3820).

23 proclaimeth (3820).

25 heaviness (3820).

13:12 sick (3820).

14:13 sorrowful (3820).

14 filled (3820).

30 sound (3820).

15:28 studieth (3820).

16:1 preparations (3820).

18:2 discover (3820).

15 prudent (3820).

19:3 fretteth (3820).

20:5 counsel (3820).

22:15 foolishness (3820).

23:7 thinketh (5315).

17 apply (3820).

17 envy (3820).

19 guide (3820).

33 perverse (3820).

24:12 pondereth (3826).

26:25 abominations

Ec. 2:10 witheld (3820).

20 despair (3820).

22 vexation (3820).

23 taketh no rest (3820).

5:2 hasty to utter (3820).

7:4 house of mirth (3820).

7 mad (3820).

26 snares and nets (3820).

8:5 discerneth (3820).

9 applied (3820).

9:1 considered (3820).

3 madness (3824).

3 full of madness and evil (3820).

10:2 wise man's heart is in his right hand (3820).

2 fools heart is in his left hand (3820).

11:9 cheer (3820).

9 ways of the heart (3820).

SofS. 4:9 ravished (3823).

Isa. 6:10 fat (3824).

7:2 moved (3824).

9:9 proud and stoutness (3824).

10:7 think (3824).

12 stout (3824).

13:7 melt (3824).

21:4 panted, fearfulness, affrighted (3824).

33:18 meditate terror (3820).

35:4 fearful (3820).

44:19 considereth (3820).

57:11 remembered (3820).

59:13 words of falsehoods (3820).

63:4 vengeance (3820).

Jer.   3:15 according (3820).
4:19 pained (3820).
5:23 revolting and rebellious (3820).
7:24 imagination (3820).
9:8 layeth in wait (7130).
14 imagination (3820).
11:8 imagination (3820).
18 imagination (3820).
13:10 imagination (3820).
16:12 imagination (3820).
17:5 departeth (3820).
9 deceitful
10 search (3820).
18:12 imagination (3820).
23:16 speak wisdom (3820).
17 imagination (3820).
20 thoughts (3820).
26 prophesy (3820).
30:24 intents (3820).
48:31 mourn (3820).
36 sound (3820).

La.   2:19 pour out (3820).
3:51 affecteth (5315).
5:17 faint (3824).
11:19 stony (3820).
14:3 set up his idols (3820).
18:31 new (3820).
22:14 endure (5315).
27:31 bitterness (5315).
33:31 covetousness (3820).
36:26 flesh (3820).

Eze.	44:7 uncircumcised (3820).
	9 uncircumcised (3820).
Da.	1:8 purposed (3820).
	2:30 thoughts (3820).
	5:22 humbled (3825).
	6:14 deliver (1079).
Ho.	7:6 made ready (3820).
	10:2 divided (3820).
	13:6 exalted (3820).
Joe.	2:13 rend (3824).

In the New Testament the meaning of the heart is in agreement with the Old Testament. In the Greek from Strong's Concordance heart is kar-dee-ah (2588). The number 2588 means thoughts, feelings, middle, heart. Funk and Wagnell's Standard Desk Dictionary defines thoughts as the act or process of using the mind actively and deliberately; meditation; cogitation. A further explanation is the product of thinking; an idea, concept, judgment, etc. It is intellectual activity of a specific kind, consideration, attention. It is an intention. Feeling means emotion, a sensation or awareness of something, sensibilities, sensitivities and desires. From the same dictionary middle is the intermediate section of the body. The heart is in the intermediate section of the body. The following is a list of scriptures that reveal just what takes place in the heart (2588).

M't. 5:8 pure.
28 adultery.
6:21 treasure.
11:29 meek and lowly.
12:34 abundance.
35 good treasure.
3:15 waxed gross.
15 understand.
19 sown.
15:8 heart is far from me.
18 those things which proceed out of the mouth come forth from the heart and they defile the man.
19 evil thoughts.
22:37 love.
24:48 say.

M'r. 6:52 hardened.
7:6 heart is far from me.
21 proceed evil thoughts, adulteries, fornications,
murders, thefts, covetousness, wickedness, deceit, lasciviousness, an evil eye, blasphemy, pride, foolishness.
8:17 hardened.
11:23 doubt.
12:30 love.

Lu. 2:19 pondered.
51 kept.
6:45 good treasure.
45 evil treasure.
45 abundance.

8:15 honest and good.

9:47 thought.

10:27 love.

12:34 treasure.

45 say.

24:25 slow of heart to believe.

32 burn.

Joh. 12:40 hardened.

40 understand.

13:2 put into.

14:1 troubled.

16:6 sorrow.

22 rejoice.

Ac. 2:26 rejoice.

37 pricked.

46 gladness and singleness.

4:32 one heart and one soul.

5:3 filled.

4 conceived.

7:51 circumcised.

54 cut to the heart.

8:21 not right.

22 thought.

37 believest.

11:23 purpose.

16:14 opened.

21:13 weep and break.

26:27 waxed.

27 understand.

Ro. 1:21 foolish heart darkened.

5 hardness and impenitent.

29 circumcision.

6:17 opened.

9:2 continual sorrow.

10:6 say.

9 believe.

10 believeth

1 Co. 7:37 standeth steadfast.

37 decreed.

14:25 secrets.

2 Co. 2:4 anguish.

3:3 fleshly tables.

15 veil.

6:11 enlarged.

8:16 earnest care.

9:7 purposeth.

Eph. 4:18 blindness.

5:19 melody.

6:5 singleness.

6 will of God (5590).

Col. 3:22 singleness of heart fearing God.

2 Th. 2:17 comfort your hearts and stablish you.

1 Tim. 1:5 pure.

2 Tim. 2:22 pure.

Heb. 3:10 err.

8 harden.

12 evil.

15 harden.

4:7 harden.

8:10 I will put my laws into their mind, and write them in their hearts.

10:16 I will put my laws into their hearts.

22 having our hearts sprinkled from an evil conscience.

Jas. 3:14 envying and strife.

4:8 purify your hearts ye double minded.

8 ye also patient; stablish your hearts.

1 Pe. 3:15 sanctify the Lord in your hearts.

2 Pe. 1:19 day star arise in your hearts.

1 Jo. 3:19 assure.

CHAPTER 5

THE MIND IS situated in the heart and is a integral part of the soul. There are many words which describe the mind. The following is an exhaustive list of definitions of the mind taken from Strong's Concordance.

1.) In the Hebrew mind is neh-fesh (5315) which means breathing creature, animal or vitality; any appetite, desire, person, pleasure, mind, heart, will.

Gen. 22:8
Dan. 18:6
1 Sam. 2:35
1 Ch. 28:9
Jer. 15:1
Eze. 28:17,18,18,22,28

2.) In the Hebrew mind is roo-akh (7307) which means spirit, but only of a rational being including it's expression and functions: courage, mind.

Gen. 26:35

Pr. 29:11
Eze. 11:5
Dan. 5:20
Hab. 1:11

3.) In the Hebrew mind is peh (6310) which means according to, command, mind.
Lev. 24:12

4.) In the Hebrew mind is labe (3820) which means feeling, the will, even intellect, mind, understanding.
Nu. 16:28
24:13
1 Sam. 9:20
Ne. 4:6
Ps. 31:12
Pr. 21:27
Isa. 3:16
65:17
Jer. 3:16
19:5
32:35
44:21
La. 3:21

5.) In the Hebrew mind is lay (3824) which means most interior, the heart, themselves, breast, mind, understanding.
1 Ch. 22:7
Jer. 51:50
Eze. 38:10
Dan. 2:29

6.) In the Hebrew mind is eem (5973) which means with in, in conjunction with, equally with, by reason of.

Job 34:33

7.) In the Hebrew mind is yay-tser (3336) which means form, conception (i.e. purpose), imagination, mind, work.

Isa. 26:3

8.) In the Greek mind is dee-an-oy-ah (1271) which means deep thought, imagination, mind, understanding.

M't. 22:37
M'r. 12:30
Lu. 10:27
12:29
Eph. 2:3
Col. 1:21
Heb. 8:10
1 Pe. 1:13

9.) In the Greek mind is an-am-im-nance-ko (363) which means to call to mind, remember, remind, recollect.

M'r. 14:72
Lu. 1:29

10.) In the Greek mind is nooce (3563) which means the intellect, i.e. mind, thought, feeling or even will and understanding.

Ro. 1:28
7:23, 25
11:34
12:2

1 Co. 1:10
2:16, 16
Eph. 4:17, 23
2 Th. 2:2
Tit. 1:15
Rev. 17:9

11.) In the Greek mind is fron-eh-o (5426) which means to exercise the mint, i.e. entertain or have a sentiment or opinion, regard, savour, think.

Ro. 8:5
12:16, 16
2 Co. 13:1
Ph'p. 2:2, 5

12.) In the Greek mind is fron-ay-mah (5427) which means inclination or purpose.

Ro. 8:7

13.) In the Greek mind is hom-oth-oo-mad-on (3661) which means unanimously-with on accord.

Ro. 15:6

14.) In the Greek mind is ep-an-ah-min-nance-ko (1878) which means to remind of, put in mind.

Ro. 15:15

15.) In the Greek mind is proth-oo-mee-ah (4288) which means predisposition, i.e. alacrity-forwardness of mind, readiness (of mind).

2 Co. 8:12, 19
9:2

16.) In the Greek mind is so-fron-eh (4993) which means to be sound mind, i.e. moderate-to be in right mind, sober (minded), soberly.

Lu. 8:35

17.) In the Greek mind is proth-oo-moce (4290) which means alacrity, willingly.

1 Pe.

18.) In the Greek mind is so-from-is-mos (4995) which means discipline, self-control, sound mind.

2 Tim. 1:7

19.) In the Greek mind is psoo-khay (5590) which means breath, animal, the rational and immortal soul, heart, life, mind, us, you.

Ph'p. 1:27

20.) In the Greek mind is tap-i-nof-ros-oo-nay (5012) which means humiliation of mind, i.e. humility (of mind), loneliness (of mind).

Ph'p. 2:3

21.) In the Greek mind is gno-may (1106) which means cognition, opinion, resolve (counsel, consent etc.): advice, judgment, mind, purpose, will.

Tit. 3:1

22.) In the Greek mind is en-noy-ah (1771) which means thoughtfulness, i.e. moral understanding-intent, mind.

1 Pe. 4:1

23.) In the Greek mind is hoop-om-im-nance-ko (5279) which means to remind quietly.

Tit. 3:1

The dictionary meaning for of mind is the aggregate of processes originating in or associated with the brain, involving conscious and subconscious thought interpretation of perceptions, insight, imagination, desire, etc. From a biblical standpoint this is not true. The mind is part of the soul, heart and spirit (which is part of the soul as it will be shown in Chapter 7).

Everyone of these definitions of the mind are attributes of the heart. In conclusion the brain is not the mind. It is a receiver of the thoughts, understanding etc. of that which is in the heart. It processes or brings together those thoughts, etc. into the natural realm. All these attributes are manifested in the brain from the blood which contains the soul. It is a mystery as to how this process occurs.

Adam had 100% capacity of his brain. It was only when his eyes were opened to evil that the brain lost a large amount of it's function. Now we only use approximately 10% of our brain. That is why the brain has trouble communicating with the heart and soul. A veil came upon the brain when sin entered Adam's life. The blood flow is still there but the veil prohibits communication of the heart and soul. The brains awareness comes from the consciousness of the heart and soul.

CHAPTER 6

NOTHER TERM FOR the heart is inward man, inward parts, inward thought, inward parts of the belly and inwardly. Job 38:36, Who hath put wisdom in the inward parts? Or who hath given understanding to the heart? Inward in Hebrew from Strong's Concordance is too-khaw (2910) which means the innermost thoughts. Parts in Hebrew from Strong's Concordance is kaw-tsaw (7098) which means the lowest, (uttermost) part. Inward parts is referring to the heart as that is where thoughts and wisdom are conceived. The heart is the innermost part of the soul as we have found in Chapter 4.

Ps. 5:9, For there is no faithfulness in their mouth; their inward part is very wickedness; their throat is an open sepulcher; they flatter with their tongue. Inward in Hebrew from Strong's Concordance is keh-reb (7130) which means the nearest part, i.e. centre, inward, within self, heart. According to Funk and Wagnell's Standard Desk Dictionary inward means toward the interior or into the mind or thoughts. The heart is the seat of emotion among other things that has already addressed in previous chapters. Within means the interior or inner part. Part in Hebrew from Strong's Concordance is khaw-tsaw (2673) which means to halve, part. Halve means to divide into two equal parts; share equally. The heart has two functions that is to maintain circulation by alternate constriction and dilation. They are equally divided or shared roles. Part also means a portion of a whole; segment. The inward part is the heart and is a part of the soul. The heart also halves equally divided roles with the spirit.

Ps. 49:11, Their inward thought is that their houses shall continue for ever, and their dwelling places to all generations; they call their lands after their own names. Inward in Hebrew from Strong's Concordance is keh-reb (7130) which means nearest part, i.e. centre, inward, within self, heart. According to Funk and Wagnell's Standard Desk Dictionary within means the inner part, interiorly, inside the body, heart or mind. The heart is the seat of emotion and its other attributes have already been discussed in previous Chapters. Thought in Hebrew from Strong's Concordance is daw-naw (1819) which means to compare, consider. Thoughts come from the heart as it has been discovered in Chapter 4. The inward thought is that which comes from the heart.

Ps. 51:6, Behold, thou desireth truth in the inward parts: and in the hidden part thou shalt make me to know wisdom. Inward in Hebrew from Strong's Concordance is too-khaw (2910) which means the innermost thoughts. Parts in Hebrew from Strong's Concordance is bad (905) which means part of the body, by self, part. Thoughts come from the heart and the heart is part of the soul.

Ps. 64:6, They search out iniquities; they accomplish a diligent search: both the inward thought of every one of them, and the heart is deep. Inward in Hebrew from Strong's Concordance is keh-der (2315) which means apartment, inner chamber, innermost, within. Funk and Wagnell's Standard Desk Dictionary defines apartment as a room. The same dictionary defines innermost as inmost; farthest within. Within has already been defined as the inner part; interior. See Ps. 5:9. Thought in Hebrew from Strong's Concordance is daw-naw (1819) which means to compare, consider. The apartment or innermost part of the body is the heart and thoughts proceed from within it.

Pr. 20:27 The spirit of man is the candle of the Lord, searching all the inward parts of the belly. Inward in Hebrew from Strong's Concordance is keh-der (2315) which means apartment, inner chamber, innermost, within. The dictionary meaning for apartment is a room. Innermost is defined as inmost; farthest within. Within is defined as the inner part; interior. Parts in Hebrew from Strong's Concordance is gheh-zer (1506) which means a portion:-part, piece. Portion denotes a part of a whole: segment. Further explanation is endowment of mind or character. Belly in Hebrew from Strong's Concordance is beh-teu (990) which means the belly, the womb, also bosom of the body of anything. Funk and Wagnell's Standard Desk Dictionary defines the bosom as the seat of thought and emotion. This is a description of some of the heart's attributes. The same dictionary defines belly as a deep, interior cavity. The inward parts of the belly is the portion or segment of the soul where thoughts and emotions are seated and that is in the heart.

Pr. 20:30, The blueness of a wound cleanseth away evil: so do stripes the inward parts of the belly. Inward in Hebrew from Strong's Concordance is keh-reb (7130) which means mearest part, i.e. center, inward, within self, heart. Inward means the heart. Parts in Hebrew from Strong's Concordance is gheh-zer (1506) means a portion:-part, piece. Portion denotes a part of a whole: segment. Belly in Hebrew from Strong's Concordance is beh-teu (990) means the belly, the womb, also the bosom of the body of anything. Bosom is defined as the seat of thought and emotion. the inward parts of the belly is the heart.

Jer. 31:33 But this shall be the covenant that I will make with the house of Israel; after those days, saith the Lord, I will put my law in their inward parts, and write it in their inward parts, and write it in their heart; and will be their God, and they shall be my people. Inward in Hebrew from Strong's Concordance is keh-reb (7130) which means the nearest part, i.e. centre, inward, within self, heart. Inward means toward the center, interior in or into the mind or thoughts. It means the heart. Center is the center or middle. Within means the inner part; interiorly, inside the body, heart or mind. Parts in Hebrew from Strong's Concordance is geh-zer (1506) which means a portion:-

part, piece. The heart is the seat of emotion, its the seat of the will and mind. The heart is the inward parts.

Luke 11:39, And the Lord said unto him, Now do ye Pharisees make clean the outside of the cup and platter; but your inward part is full of ravening and wickedness. Inward in the Greek from Strong's Concordance is es-o-then (2081) which means from inside, inward, within. Inward means the inside, center (central or middle), interior in or into the mind or thoughts. Within means inner part; interiorly, inside the body, heart or mind. Part in Greek from Strong's Concordance is mer-os (3313) which means a section or allotment. The heart is the inward part, it is the section of the soul.

Romans 7:22, For I delight in the law of God after the inward man. Inward in Greek from Strong's Concordance is es-o (2080) which means inside, within. Funk and Wagnell's Standard Desk Dictionary defines inside as that which is situated within; internal, interior. Within is the inner part; interiorly, inside the body, heart or mind. The heart is the seat of emotions and the seat of the mind and will. Man in Greek from Strong's Concordance is anth-ro-pos (444) which means the countenance, man-faced, i.e. human being:-certain, man. The inward man is the heart which is part of the soul.

2 Cor. 4:16, For which cause we faint not; but though our outward man perish, yet the inward man is renewed day by day. Inward in Greek from Strong's Concordance is es-o-then (2081) which means inside, inward, within. According to Funk and Wagnell's Standard Desk

Dictionary inward means nearest part, i.e. centre, within self. Further explanation of inward is toward the inside, center (central, middle), interior in, or into the mind or thoughts. Within means inner part; interiorly, inside the body, heart or mind. Man in Greek from Strong's Concordance is anth-ro-pos (444) which means the countenance, man-faced, i.e. human being:-certain, man. The inward man or heart is renewed day by day.

Ps. 62:4, They only consult to cast him down from his excellency: they delight in lies; they; bless with their mouth, but they curse inwardly. Selah. Inwardly in Hebrew from Strong's Concordance is keh-reh (7130) which means nearest part, the centre, inward, within self, heart. The dictionary meaning of inward is the inside, center (central, middle), interior in or into the mind or thoughts. Within means inner part, interiorly, inside the body, heart or mind. The heart is the seat of emotions, will and mind. It is the center of the soul.

M't. 7:15, Beware of false prophets which come to you in sheep's clothing but inwardly they are ravening wolves.

Inwardly in Greek from Strong's Concordance is es-o-then (2081) which means from inside:-inward, within. The dictionary meaning of inward is the nearest part, i.e. centre, inward, within self. Furthermore inward means toward the inside, center (central, middle), interior in or into the mind or thoughts. The thoughts are from the heart and the mind is seated in the heart. Within means inner part; interiorly, inside the body, heart or mind. Inwardly is referring to the heart.

The heart is the innermost part of the soul. As we have seen from study, it is the most wicked part of the man. It's where thoughts, desires, emotions, will and imaginations originate. It is the seat of the will and the mind. It ponders and meditates. The soul, which is in the blood, brings together those thoughts, etc. to the brain where they are brought into physical manifestation. The heart is the inward man, the inward parts of the belly and inwardly. The heart or inward man is renewed day by day by the spirit.

CHAPTER 7

MAN HAS A spirit. Job 32:8, But there is a spirit in man: and the inspiration of the Almighty giveth understanding. In the Hebrew from Strong's Concordance spirit is roo-akh (7307) which means wind, breath, life and by resemblance spirit, but only of a rational being (including its expressions and functions). One of the functions of the spirit is to bring inspiration to the heart and soul. The spirit is in man but where does it reside? It resides in the heart or inward man as it will be revealed in this study.

Pr. 20:27, The spirit of man is a candle of the Lord, searching all the inward parts of the belly. In Hebrew from Strong's Concordance spirit is nesh-aw-naw (5397) which means a puff, i.e. wind, vital breath, divine inspiration, intellect. Inward parts of the belly has already been in studied in Chapter 6. It means the heart or interior part of the soul. The spirit brings inspiration to the heart. Candle in Hebrew from Strong's Concordance is nay-raw (5216) which means glisten, a lamp, light. This light searches the heart. Searching in Hebrew from Strong's Concordance is khaw-fas (2664) which means to seek, conceal, change, disguise self, hide, search. The spirit is concealed or hides and changes the heart. The spirit has intelligence. This means it has reason; therefore, it is a part of the mind which is in the heart. See Chapter 5 on the mind.

Gen. 7:22, All in whose nostrils was the breath of life, of all that was in the dry land, died. In the Hebrew from Strong's Concordance breath is nesh-aw-mah (5397) which means wind, vital breath, intellect, inspiration. The breath (5397) is the same as spirit in Pr. 20:27. It is the intellect, part of the mind and the divine inspiration of the heart or inward man.

Isa. 26:9, With my soul have I desired thee in the night; yea, with my spirit within me will I seek thee early, the inhabitants of the world will learn righteousness. Here it says the spirit is within. In the Hebrew from Strong's Concordance spirit is roo-akh (7307) which means wind, breath, life and by resemblance spirit, but of a rational being (including its expressions and functions). The spirit brings inspiration, brings light and changes the heart as we have seen in Job 32:8 and Pr. 20:27. Here we see that it resides within. In the Hebrew from Strong's Concordance within is keh-rab (7130) this is the same number which means inward and inwardly (7130) in Chapter 6. Within is the inward man. The spirit resides in the inward man or heart of man.

Ps. 51:10, Create in me a clean heart, O God; and renew a right spirit within me. In the Hebrew from Strong's

Concordance spirit is roo-akh (7307) which means wind, breath, life and by resemblance spirit, but of a rational being (including its expressions and functions). The spirit is within. In the Hebrew from Strong's Concordance within is keh-rab (7130) which means inward or inwardly (7130). The inward man has been revealed to be the heart. The spirit resides within the inward man or heart.

Ps. 51:6, Behold, thou desireth truth in the inward parts: and in the hidden part thou shalt make me to know wisdom. In the Hebrew from Strong's Concordance hidden is saw-tham (5640) which means closed up, hidden, secret, shut up. In the Hebrew part is khaw-lak (2505) which means apportion, separate, part, separate self. The secret part is the spirit, it is closed up in the heart. The hidden part is the apportion of the heart.

Isa. 63:11, Then he remembered the days of old, Moses, and his people saying, where is he that brought them up out of the sea with the shepherd of his flock? Where is he that put his Holy Spirit within him? In the Hebrew from Strong's Concordance Holy Spirit is roo-akh (7307). He is a rational being with expressions and functions. He searches, changes, brings inspiration and light within. In the Hebrew from Strong's Concordance within is keh-rab (7130). The inward man, inward parts of the belly, inward thought, and inwardly are all 7130 which means heart. See Chapter 6.

Eze. 11:19, And I will give them one heart, and I will put a new spirit within you; and I will take the stony heart out of their flesh, and will give them an heart of flesh. In the Hebrew from Strong's Concordance spirit is roo-akh (7307). It is the inspiration, a light or lamp, brings changes to the heart. In the Hebrew from Strong's Concordance within is keh-rab (7130) which means the inward man (7130) or the heart.

Eze. 36:26& 27, A new heart also will I give you, and a new spirit will I put within you, and I will take away the stony heart out of your flesh, and I will give you an heart of flesh. And I will put my spirit within you, and cause you to walk in my statues, and ye shall keep my judgments, and do them. In the Hebrew from Strong's Concordance everywhere spirit is mentioned, is roo-akh (7307) which means wind, breath, life, intellect and by resemblance spirit, but only of a rational being. The spirit is a rational being. It has higher reasoning than the heart. In the Hebrew from Strong's Concordance within is keh-rab (7130) which means inward man (7130) and that has been proven to be the heart.

Zec. 12:1, The burden of the word of the Lord for Israel, saith the Lord, which stretcheth forth the heavens, and layeth the foundation of the earth, and formeth the spirit of man within him. In the Hebrew from Strong's Concordance spirit is roo-akh (7307) which means wind, breath, life, intellect and by resemblance spirit, but only of a rational being. In the Hebrew within is reh-rab (7130) which means inward man (7130) and that is the heart. Again the spirit dwells in the heart. It is inspiration, intellect, a lamp or light, it is a rational being having higher reasoning, and changes the heart of man.

1 Pe. 3:4, But let it be the hidden man of the heart, in that which is not corruptible, even the ornament of a meek and quiet spirit, which in the sight of God of great price. In the Greek from Strong's Concordance hidden is kroop-tos (2927) which means concealed, i.e. private:-hid, inwardly, secret. It is clearly stated that the hidden man is in the heart. In the Greek spirit from Strong's Concordance is pnyoo-mah (4151) which means a current of air, i.e. breath, spirit, i.e. rational soul, even the mind. The spirit is part of the mind and has higher reasoning. The spirit is part of the soul as it is in the heart and the heart is the interior of the soul.

Eph. 4:23, And be renewed in the spirit of your mind. In the Greek from Strong's Concordance spirit is pnyoo-mah (4151) which has been defined as a current of air, i.e. breath, spirit, i.e. the rational soul, even the mind. In the Greek from Strong's Concordance is nooce (3563) which means the intellect, i.e. mind, thought, feeling or will, understanding. The spirit is a part of the mind. Let the higher reasoning, that of the renewed spirit, change or bring light to your feelings, thoughts, will and understanding. The rational soul is the mind of the spirit.

Heb. 4:12, For the word of God is quick, and powerful, and sharper than any two-edged sword, piercing even to the dividing asunder of soul and spirit, and of the joints and marrow, and is a discerner of the thoughts and intents of the heart. The spirit is part of the soul, specifically, the heart (the most inward part of the soul). Soul and spirit are joined together or else it wouldn't be possible to divide them.

It has been taught that the spirit is the heart. The spirit (when it gets born again) is incorruptible so it cannot be the heart. The heart is the most wicked of all. It is by our renewed spirit and the Holy Spirit that changes come to the heart. The spirit brings light and inspiration to the heart. The spirit is the conscience of man. It reveals good from evil within the heart which is the innermost part of the soul. It renews the inward man or heart day by day. The spirit is part of the mind.

The spirit is also described as part of the mind. Gen 26:35, which were a grief of mind (7307) unto Isaac and to Rebekah. Here the word mind is translated to mean spirit. Spirit in Hebrew from Strong's Concordance is roo-akh (7307) which means breath, spirit, but only of a rational being. It possesses the faculty of reasoning just as the heart. It is part of the heart, the seat of the mind.

Pr. 29:11, A fool uttereth all his mind (7307) but a wise man keepeth it in till afterwards. Mind in Hebrew from Strong's Concordance is roo-akh (7307) which means breath, spirit, but only of a rational being. It is part of the heart, seat of the mind.

Eze. 11:5, And the spirit of the Lord fell upon me, and said unto me, Speak; Thus saith the Lord; Thus name ye said, O house of Israel: for I know the things that come into your mind, every one of them. Mind in Hebrew from Strong's Concordance is roo-akh (7307) which means breath, spirit, but only of a rational being. This rational being resides in the heart of man.

Dan. 5:20, When his heart was lifted up, and his mind hardened in pride, he was deposed from his kingly throne, and they took glory from him. Mind in Hebrew from Strong's Concordance is roo-akh (7307) which means breath, spirit, but only of a rational being. Here it is clear that the spirit is effected by sin, pride is sin.

Hab. 1:11, Then shall his mind change, and he shall pass over, and offend, imputing this his power unto his god. Mind in Hebrew from Strong's Concordance is roo-akh (7307) which means breath, spirit, but only of a rational being.

We have learned in Chapter 1 that the soul and life are the same thing but it is the spirit that gives life. Ro. 8:55, And her spirit cane again and she arose straightway: and he commanded to give her meat. Spirit in Greek from Strong's Concordance phyoo-mah (4151) which means a current of air, i.e. breath, spirit, the rational soul, vital principal, disposition, mind and life. It is part of the soul, specifically, the heart.

James 2:26, For as the body without the spirit is dead, so faith without works is dead also. Spirit in Greek from Strong's Concordance is phyoo-mah (4151) which means a current of air, i.e. breath, spirit, the rational soul, vital principal, disposition, mind and life. The life of the soul comes from the spirit.

2 Cor. 3:6 Who also hath made us able ministers of the new testament; not of the letter, but of the spirit; for the letter killeth, but the spirit giveth life. Spirit in Greeek from Strong's Concordance is phyoo-mah (4151) which means a current of air, i.e. breath, spirit, the rational soul, vital principal, disposition, mind and life. Life in Greek from Strong's Concordance is dzo-op-oy-eh-o (2227) which means vitalize:-make alive, give life, quicken. That life is in the soul, specifically, the heart. And that life comes from the spirit.

The spirit, when it is renewed or born again, is incorruptible. It dwells within the heart, the innermost part of the soul. It is a rational being or rational soul. It is intelligent and reasons. It is part of the mind. It is a lamp or light and brings changes to the heart of man. It is the hidden man of the heart. It is man's conscience. It is the inspiration of the heart and soul. It is the life of the heart, soul and of the body.

CHAPTER 8

THE SPIRIT WAS defiled when Adam sinned. 1 Co. 8:7, Howbeit there is not every man that knowledge: for some with conscience of the idol unto this hour eat it as a thing offered unto an idol; and their conscience being weak is defiled. In the Greek from Strong's Concordance weak is as-then-ace (772) which means strengthless, more feeble, impotent, sick , without, weak. In the Greek from Strong's Concordance defiled is mol-oo-no (3435) which means soil, defile.

1 Co. 8:10, For if any man see thee which hast knowledge sit at meat in the idol's temple, shall not the conscience of him which is weak be emboldened to eat those things which are offered to idols. In the Greek from Strong's Concordance weak is as-then-o (770) which means feeble, diseased, impotent, sick, weak. In the Greek from Strong's Concordance emboldened is oy-kod-om-eh-o (3618) which means embolden, construct, give courage to, confirm.

1 Co. 8:12, But when ye sin so against the brethren, and wound their weak conscience, ye sin against Christ. In the Greek from Strong's Concordance weak is as-then-eh-o (770) which means feeble, disased, impotent, sick, weak.

Tit. 1:15, Unto the pure all things are pure: but unto them that are defiled and unbelieving is nothing pure; but even their mind and conscience is defiled. In the Greek form Strong's Concordance defiled is me-ah-ee-no (3392) which means to sully or taint, i.e. contaminate, defile, tarnish, blemish. In the Greek from Strong's Concordance mind is nooce (3563) which means the intellect, i.e. mind, thought, feeling or will, understanding.

Heb. 9:14, How much more shall the blood of Christ, who through the eternal Spirit offered himself without spot to God, purge your conscience from dead works to serve the living God? In the Greek from Strong's Concordance purge is kath-ar-id-zo (2511) which means to cleanse, clean, purge, purify. In the Greek from Strong's Concordance dead is mek-ros (3498) which means dead, i.e. lifeless, no longer in force. In the Greek from Strong's Concordance works is yoo-por-eh-o (2041) which means toil, an act or deed, labour.

Heb. 10:22, Let us draw near with a true heart in full assurance of faith, having our hearts sprinkled from an evil conscience, and our bodies washed with pure water. In the Greek from Strong's Concordance hearts is kar-dee-ah (2588) which means the heart, i.e. the thoughts or feelings (mind). In the Greek from Strong's Concordance sprinkled is hran-tid-zo (4472) which means to render besprinkled, i.e. asperse, sprinkle. To scatter in drops or small particles. In the Greek from Strong's Concordance evil is pon-ay-nos (4190) which means hurtful, i.e. evil, diseased, malicious, bad. The heart is effected by and evil conscience.

In all of the verses mentioned conscience in the Greek from Strong's Concordance is soon-i-day-sis (4893) which means co perception, i.e. moral consciousness, conscience. Conscience is the faculty by which distinctions are made between moral right and wrong. It is a part of the spirit. It is the knowledge or insight of the spirit in communication with the heart and soul. In these verses the conscience is defiled, weak, impotent, sick, evil, malicious and gives false courage to the heart. It is no longer in force to do what it was created to do. The heart is in need of circumcision and the spirit needs rebirth or renewing.

CHAPTER 9

WHEN ADAM ATE from the tree of the knowledge of good and evil he sinned against God. He opened his heart, soul and spirit to darkness. As a result it brought death to the body. Be he slew not their children, but did as it is written in the law in the book of Moses, where the Lord commanded saying, The fathers shall not die for the children, neither shall the children die for the fathers, but every man shall die for his own sin. 2 Ch. 25:4. But of the tree of the knowledge of good and evil, thou shalt not eat of it: for the day that thou eatest thereof thou shalt surely die. Gen. 2:17. The wages of sin is death; but the gift of God is eternal life through Jesus Christ our Lord. Ro. 6:23.

Adam's sin corrupted the heart to work wickedness. Ps. 58:2. The heart is in need of salvation. It has a foreskin. It is in need of circumcision. Circumcise therefore the foreskin of your heart, and be no more stiffnecked. De. 10:16. In that ye have brought into my sanctuary strangers, uncircumcised in heart, and uncircumcised in flesh, to be in my sanctuary, to pollute it, even my house when ye off my bread, the fat and the blood, and they have broken my covenant because of all your abominations. Eze. 44:7. Thus saith the Lord God; No stranger uncircumcised in heart, nor uncircumcised in flesh, shall enter into my sanctuary, of any stranger that is among the children of Israel. Eze. 44:9. And the Lord thy God will circumcise thine heart, and the heart of thy seed, to love the Lord with all thine heart, and with all thy soul, that thou mayest live. De. 30:6.

Circumcision of the heart (3824-mind) is a change of mind to love and do what is right and keep the commandments of the Lord. The uncircumcised heart (3820-will) is willful to the things against God's commandments. In the Old Testament it meant to follow the law of Moses but in the New Testament it means to follow Jesus Christ. But he is a Jew, which is one inwardly; and circumcision is that of the heart, in the spirit, and not of the letter, whose praise is not of men, but of God. Ro. 2:29. Here heart is 2588 which means the heart, i.e. thoughts or feelings. It is speaking of the mind. It further states, in the spirit. The circumcision of the heart goes into the mind of the spirit. It is a cutting into the mind of the heart and spirit to recreate it. And be renewed in the spirit of your mind. Eph. 4:23. The mind of the heart and of the spirit is changed when the heart is circumcised.

The heart becomes clean and the spirit is renewed when the heart is circumcised. Create in me a clean heart, O God; and renew a right spirit within me. Ps. 51:10. In the Hebrew from Strong's Concordance renew is khaw-dash (2318) which means renew or rebuild, restore to former condition. In the Hebrew from Strong's Concordance right is koon (3559) which means to be erect, be stable, perfect. The spirit becomes perfect and stable when it is renewed. Cast away from you all your transgressions, whereby ye have transgressed; and make you a new heart and a new spirit: for why will ye die, O house of Israel? Eze 18:31. New is something that never existed or occured before. I will put a new spirit within you. Eze. 11:19. Here new is the same as in Eze. 18:31. A new heart also will I give you, and a new spirit will I put within you: Eze. 36:29. New means the same thing as it does in Eze. 18:31. Upon circumcision of the heart or rebirth. We become new creations with clean hearts and new spirits. We should serve in newness of spirits. Ro. 7:6.

The state of the clean heart is conditional because of the will. The heart is in a constant state of renewing. For which cause we faint not; but though our outward man perish, yet the inward man is renewed day by day. 2 Co. 4:16. Inward is referring to the heart as it has already been discussed. And be not conformed to this world: but be ye transformed by the renewing of your mind, that ye may prove what is good, and perfect, will of God. Ro. 12:2. Not by works of righteousness which we have done, but according to his mercy he saved us, by the washing of regeneration, and renewing of the Holy Ghost. Tit. 3:5. Salvation is a work in progress. Wherefore, my beloved, as ye have always obeyed, not as in my presence only but only, but now much more in my absence, work out your own salvation with fear and trembling. Ph'p. 2:12. There is a growing process as the heart surrenders to the Holy Spirit.

CHAPTER 10

EVEN AFTER THE heart is circumcised it still has frailties or passions called the flesh. They are ungodly lusts which are immoderate desires, usually for that which is forbidden. Those desires are external, temporal and only pertain to the affairs of the present life. The flesh is setting one's desires on those things which only last for a season. They are not spiritual.

There is therefore no condemnation to them which are in Christ Jesus, who walk not after the flesh, but after the Spirit. Ro. 8:1. We are to follow the Spirit of God and then we'll overcome the works of the flesh. This I say then, walk in the Spirit, and ye shall not fulfil the lust of the flesh. For the flesh lusteth against the Spirit, and the Spirit against the flesh: and these are contrary to one to the other: so that ye cannot do the things that ye would. Ga. 5:16-17. And they that are Christ's have crucified the flesh with the affections and lusts. Ga.5:24. We are to impale or extinguish the lusts of the flesh.

The will has to be conformed to that of the Spirit. Watch and pray, that ye enter not into temptation: the spirit is willing, but the flesh is weak. M't. 26:41. The flesh influences the will being rooted in impure thoughts, motives and desires. For though we walk in the flesh, we do not war after the flesh: (For the weapons of our warfare are not carnal, but mighty through God to the pulling down of strongholds;) casting down imaginations and every high thing that exaleth itself against the knowledge of God, and bringing into captivity every thought to the obedience of Christ. 2 Co. 10:4-5.

Our affections should be set on charity not the flesh. Charity overcomes the manifestation of fleshly lusts. Charity suffereth long, and is kind, charity vaunteth not itself, is not puffed up, doth not behave itself unseemly, seeketh not her own, is not easily provoked, thinketh no evil; Rejoiceth not in iniquity, but rejoiceth in truth; Beareth all things, endureth all things. Charity never faileth. 1 Co. 13:4-8.

BIBLIOGRAPHY

Revelation Seminar Holy Bible, King James Version 1976 Today Inc.

Strong's Exhaustive Concordance of the Bible By James Strong S.T.D., L.L.D.

Funk and Wagnell's Standard Desk Dictionary volume 1 and 2. copyright 1964, 1966, 1969, 1977, 1980, 1984 by Harper and Row, Publishers, Inc.